A Far Side collection

THE CHICKENS ARE

RESTLESS

Other Books in The Far Side Series

The Far Side
Beyond The Far Side
In Search of The Far Side
Bride of The Far Side
Valley of The Far Side
It Came From The Far Side
Hound of The Far Side
The Far Side Observer
Night of the Crash-Test Dummies
Wildlife Preserves
Wiener Dog Art
Unnatural Selections
Cows of Our Planet

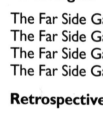

Anthologies

The Far Side Gallery
The Far Side Gallery 2
The Far Side Gallery 3
The Far Side Gallery 4

Retrospective

The PreHistory of The Far Side: A 10th Anniversary Exhibit

A Far Side collection by Gary Larson

THE CHICKENS ARE

RESTLESS

SCHOLASTIC INC.
New York Toronto London Auckland Sydney

THE FAR SIDE is distributed internationally by Universal Press Syndicate.

Printed on recycled paper.

ISBN 0-590-47987-3

12 11 10 9 8 7 6 5 4 3 2 1   4 5 6 7 8 9/9

Printed in the U.S.A.   02

First Scholastic printing, January 1994

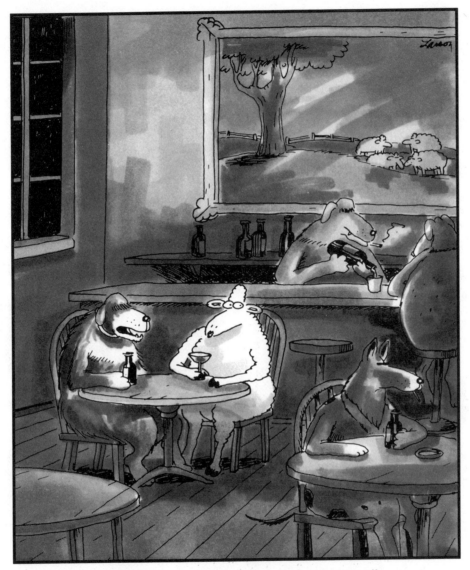

"Confession time, Mona: I've led you astray."

"Mmmmmm ... interesting ... interesting. ... I'd say we taste a little like chicken."

And for the rest of his life, Ernie told his friends that he had talked with God.

To the horror of the lifeboat's other members,
Madonna loses her balance and falls on her face.

Fumbling for his recline button, Ted
unwittingly instigates a disaster.

"God, Collings, I hate to start a Monday
with a case like this."

At Slow Cheetahs Anonymous

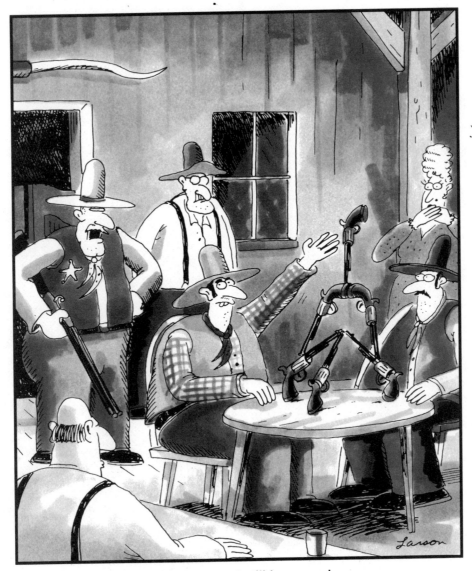

"OK, boys — that'll be enough.
We don't allow any gunplay in this town."

"OK, time for lunch. ... And Dwayne here will
be dismissing you by row number,
since he's alpha wolf today."

The living hell of Maurice, Jacques Cousteau's cat

Red Cloud's ultimate nightmare

"I'm afraid we're going to have to head back, folks. ...
We've got a warning light on up here, and darn
if it isn't the big one."

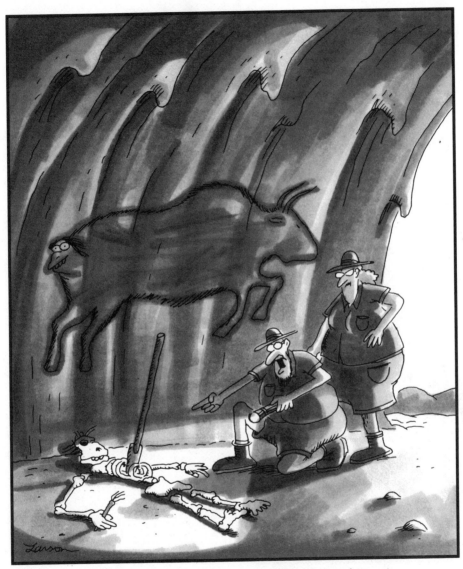

"Amazing! The mummified remains of a prehistoric
cave-painter — still clutching his brush! ...
Seems he made an enemy, though."

The Viking longcar was once the scourge of European roadways.

A Louvre guard is suddenly unsettled by
the arrival of Linda Blair.

"Remember, Calloway, this is their biggest and best
warrior — so stay alert! When you knock him
down, he's going to come right back at you!"

Origin of the expression, "Putting on the dog"

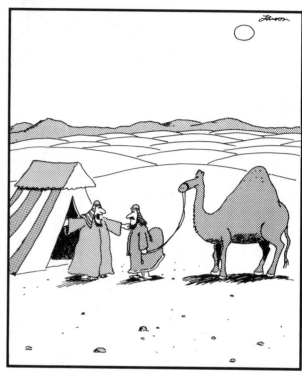

"Abdul, my old friend! Come in! Come in! Have you traveled far?!"

Hummingbirds, of course, have to watch nature films
with the action greatly speeded up.

"As you can see, most of these things are jackrabbits, but keep your eyes peeled for armadillo as well. ... We're about five miles now from the dead steer."

Although never achieving the fame of his African counterpart, Larry of the Lemurs was a common sight to natives of Madagascar.

Bored dogs are often subject to the phenomenon of cat mirages.

Pickpockets of the Rue Morgue

Tarantula coffeehouses

"OK, Mr. Hook. Seems you're trying to decide between a career in pirating or massage therapy. Well, maybe we can help you narrow it down."

"We can't go on like this, Ramone. ... One day, George is bound to take his blinders off."

With the surgical team passed out, and with help from the observation deck, hospital custodian Leonard Knudson suddenly became responsible for bringing Mr. Gruenfeld "home."

"Well, there goes Binky with the boss again. ... What a red-noser!"

"*His* story? Well, I dunno. ... I always assumed he was just a bad dog."

She was known as Madame D'Gizarde, and, in the early '40s, she used deceit, drugs, and her beguiling charms to become the bane of chicken farmers everywhere.

Scene from *Dr. Jekyll and Mr. Ed*

Again the doorbell chimed. With his wife out of town, and not expecting any visitors, Mohammed began to grow uneasy.

Popeye on the dating scene

Wellington held out some beads and other trinkets, but the islanders had sent their fiercest lawyers — some of whom were chanting, "Sue him! Sue him!"

Trouble brewing

The writers for "Bewitched" sit down to their
weekly brainstorming session.

Every August, the fleas would test their endurance
in the grueling Tour de Frank.

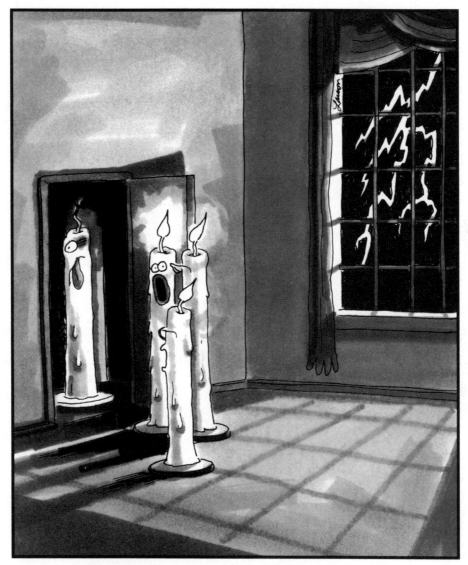

"AAAAAAAAAA! It's Sid! Someone snuffed him!"

As witnesses later recalled, two small dogs just waltzed into the place, grabbed the cat, and waltzed out.

Where the respective worlds of boating and herpetology converge.

Testifying before a Senate subcommittee,
the Hardy boys crack the Iran-contra scandal.

"Go ahead and jump, Sid! Hell — I *know* you're
thinkin' it!"

"Oh, it's just Hank's little cross to bear — he's allergic to down and that's that."

As his eyes grew accustomed to the dark, Death suddenly noticed his girlfriend sitting with Dr. Jack Kevorkian.

Every year, hundreds of tourists travel great distances to get a glimpse of the few remaining mountain chihuahuas.

The curse of songwriter's block

"Now now now. ... You won't be a lonely road
forever, you know."

The ever-popular Donner Party snow dome

Long before his show-business career, he was known as Mr. Liberace, the wood-shop teacher.

"Well, I'll be. ... I must've been holding the dang work order like *this*!"

It was always a bizarre spectacle, but no one ever,
ever, ridiculed the Teapot Kid.

"OK, ma'am you said you warned your husband to
put the newspaper down or you'd blow him away. ...
Did he respond?"

And then the bovine watchers were given a *real* treat. On a small knoll, in full splendor, there suddenly appeared a Guatemalan cow of paradise.

"Boy, everyone's really out wandering the streets tonight. ... I tell you, Charles, we're getting to be real home zombies."

Monday night in the woods

Moses parting his hair

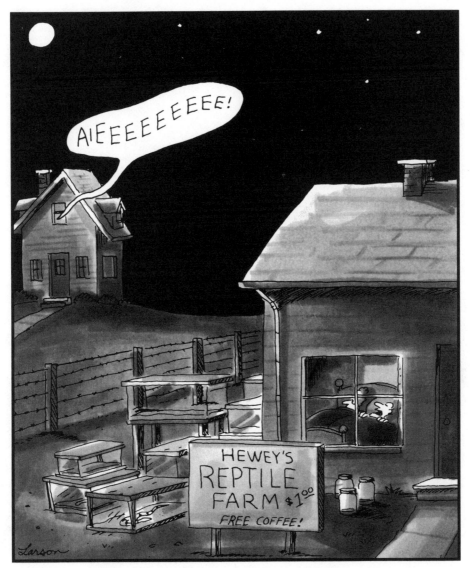

"We're screwed, Marge. Big Al was our star attraction, the king of the show. ... And now he's gone."

Unbeknownst to most students of psychology,
Pavlov's first experiment was to ring a bell and cause
his dog to attack Freud's cat.

"Don't touch it, honey ... it's just a face
in the crowd."

It was a tough frontier town; but later,
after the arrival of the Earp brothers, things calmed
down, and the town's name was shortened to
simply Dodge City.

The Angel of Migraines

"Hey, Lola. Did you see this thing in the paper?"

Question: If a tree falls in the forest and no one's
around, and it hits a mime, does anyone care?

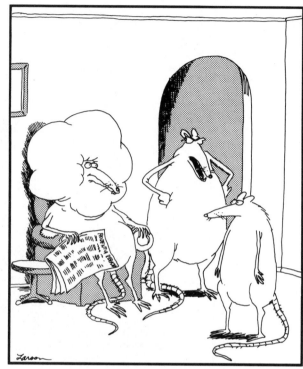

"Quit school? *Quit school?* You wanna end up
like your father? A career lab rat?"

A tragedy occurs off the coast of a land called
Honah-Lee.

"Edgar! Leave him be! ... Always best to let
sleeping dogs lie."

Ichabod Crane vs. the Headless Horseman
in The People's Court

"Well, kid, ya beat me — and now every punk
packin' a paddle and tryin' to make a name
for himself will come lookin' for *you*! ...
Welcome to hell, kid!"

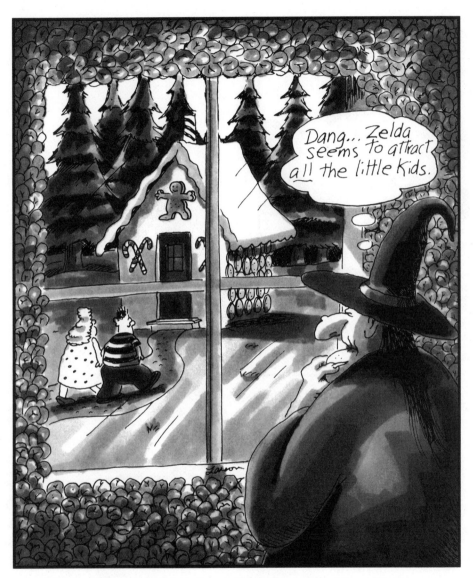

Later, Edna was forced to sell her brussels sprout house.

Years later, Harold Zimmerman, the original
"Hookhand" of the campfire ghost stories, tells his
grandchildren the Tale of the Two Evil Teen-agers.

Suddenly, the cops stepped into the clearing, and
the Spamshiners knew they were busted.

"Dogs that drink from the toilet bowl — after this."

The woods were dark and foreboding,
and Alice sensed that sinister eyes were watching
her every step. Worst of all, she knew that
Nature abhorred a vacuum.

Early plumbers

Chicken sexual fantasies

"Sheriff! Ben Wiggins is ridin' into town, and he's wearin' that same little chiffon number that he wore when he shot Jake Sutton!"

Scene from *Insurance Salesman of the Opera*

"Little Bear! A watched head never gets eaten by ants."

Historical note: For many years, until they became truly nasty, Vikings would plunder, loot, and then egg the houses of coastal villagers.

Hot off the press, the very first edition of the *Desert Island Times* caused the newspaper to quickly fold.

"Oo! *I'd* get up on that big fuzzy one!"

"So Mr. Pig — you built that fire *after* you heard my client coming down your chimney! ... Did you know my client is an endangered species, Mr. Pig, while you yourself are nothing more than a walking side of ham?"

The magnificent Lippizaner cows

Tapeworms on vacation

"Oh, the box of dead flies? Ramone gave them to me
Saturday night during his courtship display. ... Of
course they were already sucked dry."

"Look, if it was electric, could I do this?"

"It's time we face reality, my friend. ... We're not exactly rocket scientists."

Octopus obedience school

Calf delinquents

Jurassic calendars

Cossaccountants

"And then wham! This thing just came right
out of left field."

Be a virus, see the world.

On this particular day, Rory the raccoon was hunting frogs at his favorite stream, and the pleasant background music told him that Mr. Mountain Lion was nowhere around.

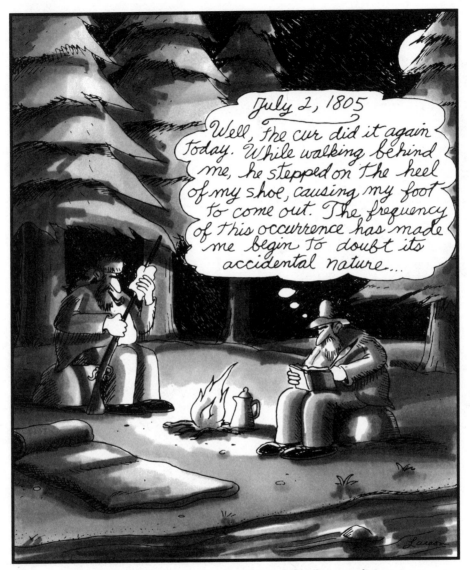

Tensions mount on the Lewis and Clark expedition.

Only Claire, with her oversized brain, wore an
expression of concern.

"Excuse me, sir, but could your entire family please
step out of the car? ... Your faces are not in order."

"Norm? This is Mitch. ... You were right —
I found my drill."

In her past, and unbeknownst to most people, Leona Helmsley was an avid bungee jumper.

Near misses of the Old West

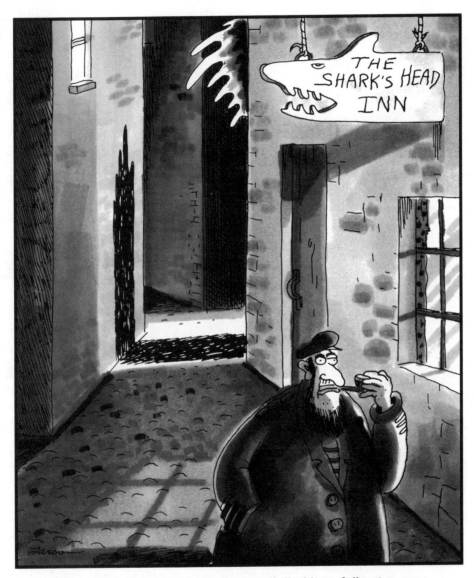

That night, Captain MacIntyre was killed by a following sea.

"Hey, boy! How ya doin'? ... Look at him, Dan.
Poor guy's been floating out here for days but
he's still just as fat and happy as ever."

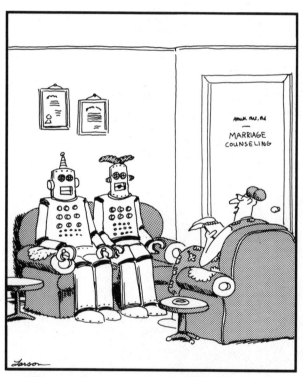

"The problem, as I see it, is that you both are
extremely adept at pushing each other's buttons."

Through mostly grunts and exaggerated gestures,
two fishermen/gatherers attempt to communicate.

More facts of nature: All forest animals, to this very
day, remember exactly where they were and what
they were doing when they heard that Bambi's
mother had been shot.

Sorry, your highness, but you're really not the dictator of Ithuvania, a small European republic. In fact, there is no Ithuvania. The hordes of admirers, the military parades, this office -- we faked it all as an experiment in human psychology. In fact, your highness, your real name is Edward Belcher, you're from Long Island, New York, and it's time to go home, Eddie.

"One more time: You were at the park, enjoying the afternoon, when you distinctly heard the defendant turn to his dog and say: 'Look, boy! A stickman!'"

Zoombies: the driving dead

"Hey, who's that? ... Oh — Mitch, the janitor. Well,
our first test run has just gotten a little more
interesting."

Drive-by erasings

"He kids me ... he kids me not. ... He kids me ...
he kids me not. ..."

"In this dramatic turn of events, testimony against
Mr. Pumpkineater is about to be given by his sister,
Jeannie Jeannie Eatszucchini."

"Professor LaVonne had many enemies in the entomological world, detective, but if you examine that data label, you'll find exactly when and where he was — shall we say — 'collected.'"

Failed marketing ploys

What the stranger didn't know, of course, was that Sam
always kept a dobie in his boot.

"Well, lemme think. ... You've stumped me, son.
Most folks only wanna know how to go
the other way."

Back in his college days, Igor was considered to be
the HBOC.

"Hey! You're not lookin' to buy anything, are you?
I think you best just keep movin', buddy."

"Oh, my God! Dung beetles! ... And in their
filthy dungarees, of course!"

"Of course, one of the more popular myths is that our 16th president was born in a little log cabin."

"OK, OK! Calm down, everyone! ... This monster — would you say he was bigger or smaller than your building? ... You can talk it over."

Henry VIII on the dating scene

He had seen Tanzania, and most of Mozambique was
already behind him. There was no mistake. Chippy
had done what most chimps only dream about:
He had caught the Perfect Vine.

"I love the desert."

Careening through the neighborhood with
reckless abandon, none of them suspected that
Tuffy was still tied up.

"You *must* be new here! ... That's Miss Crutchfield,
and she's there to make sure *nobody*
runs with scissors."

"Tell me, Margaret. ... Am I a butthead?"

"Thanks for being my friend, Wayne."

Common butt stickers of the Old West

At the I've Fallen and I Can't Get Up Building

Abducted by an alien circus company,
Professor Doyle is forced to write calculus
equations in center ring.

Boxer nightmares

It was no place for yellow squash.

"This is it, Maurice! I've warned you to keep your hens off me!"

"Hey! You! ... Yeah, you! I ain't gonna tell you again
to quit spittin' on me!"

Early corsages

He was king of the sheep.

"Whoa whoa whoa, young man! You *walk* the plank like everyone else!"

A big day for Jimmy

Only Bernard, in the front row, had the nerve to laugh at Death.

"Be patient, Leona, be patient. ... Zebras won't take
a drink until they know it's absolutely safe."

Long before his rise to fame, artist Gus Nickerson
experimented with many variations on a single
theme — until that fateful day when a friend said,
"Gus ... have you tried *dogs* playing poker?"

"And so," the interviewer asked,
"do you ever have trouble coming up with ideas?"
"Well, sometimes," the cartoonist replied.